IT'S TYRANNOSAURUS REX!

by Dawn Bentley
Illustrated by Karen Carr

For Tyler William. Love, Aunt Dawn. — D.B.

Dedicated with love to my husband, Ralph, and daughter, Jo. — K.C.

Book design: Marcin D. Pilchowski
Editor: Laura Gates Galvin
Editorial assistance: Chelsea Shriver

First Edition 2003
10 9 8 7 6 5 4 3 2
Printed in China

Acknowledgements:
    Our very special thanks to Dr. Brett-Surman of the Smithsonian Institution's National Museum of Natural History.
    Soundprints would like to thank Ellen Nanney and Katie Mann of the Smithsonian Institution for their help in the creation of the book.

IT'S TYRANNOSAURUS REX!

by Dawn Bentley
Illustrated by Karen Carr

Soundprints
Where Children Discover...

The ancient forest is filled with peaceful sounds of prehistoric life—birds are chirping, insects are buzzing, and animals are splashing in a stream. Suddenly, there is a loud pounding sound. The once calm forest now fills with alarmed cries as animals hurry into hiding.

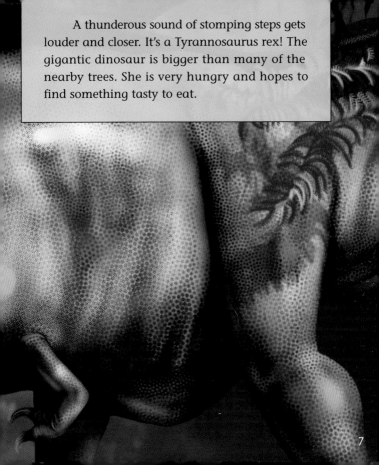

A thunderous sound of stomping steps gets louder and closer. It's a Tyrannosaurus rex! The gigantic dinosaur is bigger than many of the nearby trees. She is very hungry and hopes to find something tasty to eat.

8

Tyrannosaurus rex opens her giant mouth and snaps her 60 dagger-like teeth at a Quetzalcoatlus gliding by. She grunts in anger as she watches the reptile flap its long wings and fly away.

Tyrannosaurus rex sniffs the air with her powerful nose. She smells lunch! She searches the land with her large, keen eyes. She sees something moving on the other side of the stream.

11

She walks on her toes into the water, leaving a trail of huge footprints on the muddy banks. As Tyrannosaurus rex splashes her way across, she almost steps on a crocodile hiding in the reeds!

She sees a Triceratops in the distance. She chases him with her long, stiff tail pointing straight out behind her to help her stay balanced. Without it, she would fall over! Within seconds, she catches up to the Triceratops.

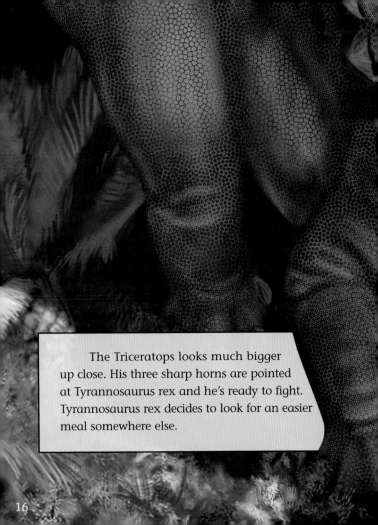

The Triceratops looks much bigger up close. His three sharp horns are pointed at Tyrannosaurus rex and he's ready to fight. Tyrannosaurus rex decides to look for an easier meal somewhere else.

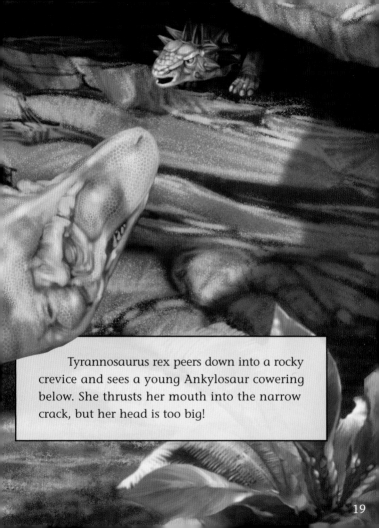

Tyrannosaurus rex peers down into a rocky crevice and sees a young Ankylosaur cowering below. She thrusts her mouth into the narrow crack, but her head is too big!

Frustrated, Tyrannosaurus rex tries to squeeze her head down farther into the crevice. Her hot breath blows down on the Ankylosaur as she gets closer. Tyrannosaurus rex snaps at the young dinosaur, but she misses.

Tyrannosaurus rex snaps at the baby again, this time biting into a jagged rock. Crack! She breaks her tooth! She pushes her head down as far as it will go, but she still can't reach the baby.

Tyrannosaurus rex soon finds a meal elsewhere. She chases a small Anatotitan. Tyrannosaurus rex grabs him with her powerful jaw. It took all day to find lunch, but at last she gets to eat.

25

Suddenly, a loud rumbling sound startles Tyrannosaurus rex! It's the sound of a volcano about to erupt.

Tyrannosaurus rex might be the fiercest predator in all the land, but a volcano is more powerful than she is! She hurries away in search of a place where she can once again be the most powerful thing of all.

ABOUT THE TYRANNOSAURUS REX
(tye-RAH-nuh-saur-us rex)

It has been about 65 million years since Tyrannosaurus rex roamed the earth. They lived during a time known as the Cretaceous period. Tyrannosaurus rex were the biggest meat-eating dinosaurs to live on land. They were as tall as a two-story building—their legs alone were 10-feet high and they could be as long as a school bus! A Tyrannosaurus rex weighed up to eight tons—that is more than two large elephants! They had very big heads with giant mouths that had about 60 sharp teeth that could grow to be 8 inches long. It would take about 32 of your teeth to equal the length of one Tyrannosaurus rex tooth!

Tyrannosaurus rex weren't just big. They had a keen sense of smell, they had good eyesight, and they could move quickly. All of these qualities made the Tyrannosaurus rex a great hunter.

PICTORIAL GLOSSARY

▲ Tyrannosaurus rex

▲ Ankylosaur

▲ **Anatotitan**

▲ **Triceratops**

▲ Crocodile

▲ Quetzalcoatlus

▲ **Hypsilophodons**

▲ **Prehistoric mammal**